YOUR FAVORITE STARS

FEATURING

SELENA GOMEZ

FACTS, QUIZZES, ACTIVITIES, AND MORE!

by Erin Falligant

CAPSTONE PRESS
a capstone imprint

This is an unauthorized biography.

Published by Capstone Press, an imprint of Capstone
1710 Roe Crest Drive, North Mankato, Minnesota 56003
capstonepub.com

Library of Congress Cataloging-in-Publication Data is available on the Library of Congress website.
ISBN: 9798875255205 (hardcover)
ISBN: 9798875255151 (paperback)
ISBN: 9798875255168 (ebook PDF)

Summary: A collection of fun facts, quizzes, and activities featuring the singing and acting superstar Selena Gomez.

Editorial Credits
Editor: Carrie Sheely; Designer: Elijah Blue; Media Researcher: Rebekah Hubstenberger; Production Specialist: Tori Abraham

Image Credits
Getty Images: Amy Sussman, 18, Andreas Rentz, 31 (bottom), Christopher Polk for Sony Pictures Entertainment, 16, Cindy Ord for Coach, 37 (top right), Craig Barritt for Serendipity3, 39 (bottom), David Livingston, 12, Emma McIntyre, 21, 39 (top), Gareth Cattermole, 5 (middle), Jeff Spicer for BFI, 11, Joe Corrigan, 43 (bottom), John Shearer for MTV, 27, Jon Kopaloff, 47, Kate Green, 6 (right), Kevin Winter, cover, Kevork Djansezian, 19 (right), Larry Busacca, 37 (left), Mat Hayward for Netflix, 9, Matt Winkelmeyer, 17, 33, Mike Coppola for Rare Beauty, 35 (left), Monica Schipper for Rare Impact Fund, 41, NBC Television/Handout, 15 (bottom right), Presley Ann for DAOU Vineyards, 25, Tasos Katopodis for MTV Entertainment, 40, Tommaso Boddi for WE, 45; Newscom: 20TH CENTURY FOX TELEVISION/Album, 15 (top right), DISNEY CHANNEL/Album, 13, July Moon Productions, 29; Shutterstock: ANNA ZASIMOVA (rainbow chrome star), back cover, 47, BlackWhiteMouse Design, 6 (smartphone), derter (rainbow chrome sparkle), back cover, 39, freshcare, 35 (makeup), GN.Studio, 14 (sneaker), GreenSkyStudio, 14 (overalls), katillomi, cover (lipstick), Kucher Serhii, 46, lanastace, 43 (middle right), Mashaart (silver star), back cover and throughout, Monkichi Lutwidge, 37 (middle right), Natykach Nataliia, 31 (chef hat), Net Vector, 19 (green slime), New Africa, 30, nopparada samrhubsuk, cover (cooking glove), PxB, 5 (heart chat icon), 38 (music notes), Rina Antipina, 15 (bikini), Rokas Tenys, 22, topseller, 31 (cookies), v_kulieva (blurry heart background), cover and throughout, Vlas Telino studio (vinyl record), front cover, 20

Printed and bound in China. 006461

TABLE OF

CONTENTS

CHAPTER 1

A POP ICON

Singer. Actor. Producer. Businesswoman. Is there anything **SELENA GOMEZ** can't do? She made magic as a child actor on ***Wizards of Waverly Place***. She signed her first record deal by age 16. And after founding her own makeup line, **Rare Beauty**, she became one of the world's youngest self-made billionaires! Fans adore her because she knows how to keep it real. She's open about her physical and mental health struggles, and she uses her fame to give back to people in need.

STAR SCOOP!

Selena has made her singing and acting dreams come true, but she said her *biggest* dream is "to make a positive impact in this world."

FOLLOWERS BY THE NUMBERS

In 2025, Selena was the second most followed person across social media with more than 685 million followers! She has also been named one of the most positive influencers in the world. Now that's a star worth following.

STAR SCOOP!

In September 2016, Selena became the first person to reach 100 million followers on Instagram. She won a Guinness World Record for reaching the milestone! And in March 2023, she became the first woman to reach 400 million followers on Instagram.

In 2025, Selena had oodles of followers on every major social media platform. Check out these numbers!

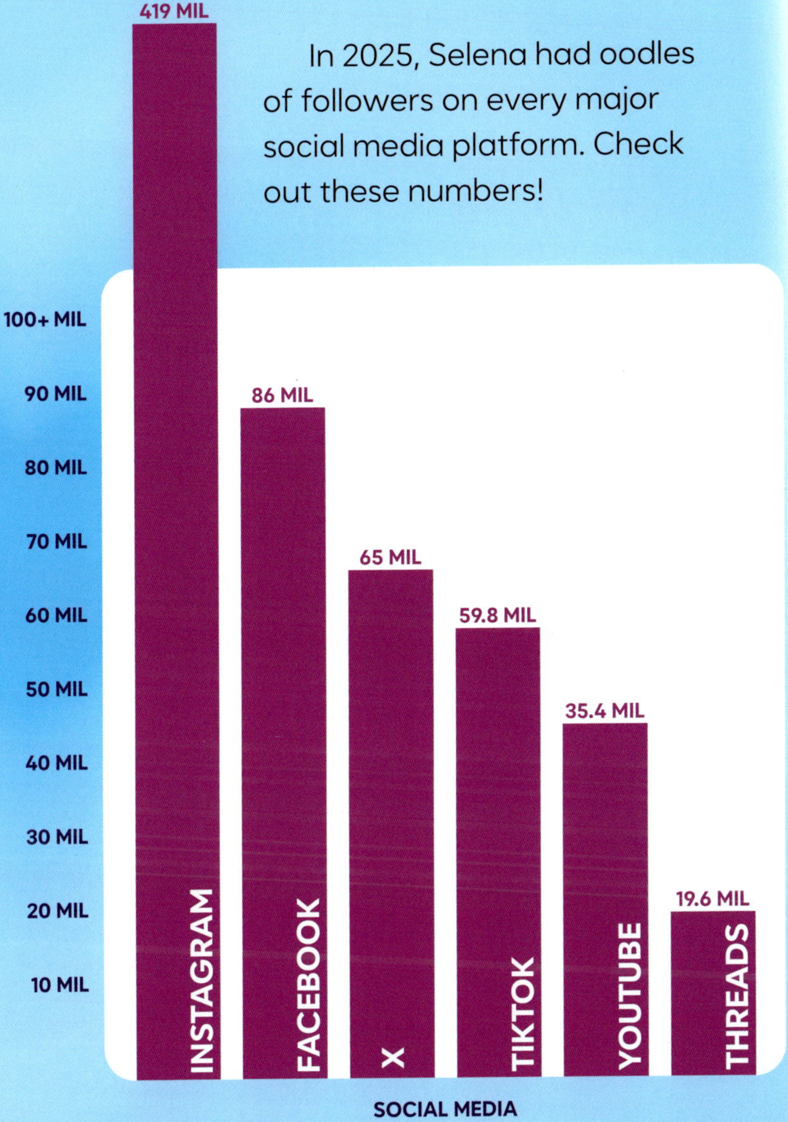

THE SELENATORS

Selena's official fan club is called "the Selenators." Nominated three times as the "Fiercest Fans" by the Radio Disney Music Awards, the Selenators have supported Selena through highs and lows. If Selena cares about a cause, the Selenators do too! They've donated to the **UNITED NATIONS CHILDREN'S FUND (UNICEF)** and supported her work in mental health awareness. When Selena turned 30, she gave her fans a tearful shout-out on TikTok. She thanked them for "being in my life" and "for growing up with me."

STAR SCOOP!

Selena is a fangirl too! Some of the stars she has admired are **Christina Aguilera**, **Britney Spears**, **Beyoncé**, **Rihanna**, **Taylor Swift**, **Billie Eilish**, and **Bruno Mars**.

quiz!

TRUE OR FALSE?

How much do you know about Selena? Decide which of these statements are true and which are false.

1. Selena was born in Grande Prairie, Texas.
2. Her parents came to the U.S. from Mexico.
3. Selena was named after a singer.
4. She spoke Spanish at home growing up.
5. Selena was really outgoing in school.

6. Selena named her cats Winnie and Daisy.

7. Her favorite color is red.

Answers: 1. True. 2. False. Her grandparents came from Mexico. 3. True. She was named after Selena Quintanilla-Pérez. 4. True. 5. False. She was super shy! 6. False. Those are her poodles! 7. False. It's green.

CHAPTER 2

ON-SCREEN SENSATION

Selena didn't have to look far to find role models for her acting career. Her mom, Mandy Teefey, was a stage actor. She inspired Selena to audition for roles too. At the age of 10, Selena got her first regular gig playing **GIANNA** on ***Barney & Friends***. Selena said, "I was proud because I got to go escape my life and be in Barney Land and just play and sing."

But which role made Selena famous? That was **ALEX RUSSO** on Disney's ***Wizards of Waverly Place***. Selena waved her wand, and magic happened—on set and in her career.

Mandy Teefey

Selena on the set of *Wizards of Waverly Place*

STAR SCOOP!

Alex Russo wasn't Selena's first role on the Disney channel. She started out with smaller roles on ***The Suite Life of Zack & Cody*** and ***Hannah Montana.***

COSTUME CHANGES

How does Selena get into character? By making careful choices about what her characters would wear!

Gianna in ***Barney & Friends***: **T-shirts and shorts or overalls**

Alex in *Wizards of Waverly Place*: layered tops with colorful leggings or skinny jeans

Mikayla in *Hannah Montana*: brightly colored shirts, vests, and hats

Beezus in *Ramona and Beezus*: sweaters, layered tops, and jeans

Dot in *The Fundamentals of Caring*: jeans, T-shirts, hoodies, and sneakers

Mary in *Another Cinderella Story*: skater-style dark, baggy clothes

Mabel in ***Only Murders in the Building***: bright coats, sweaters, and plaid skirts or pants

Faith in ***Spring Breakers***: swimsuits and shorts

Jessi in ***Emilia Pérez***: fancy dresses and a fur coat

Selena in *Only Murders in the Building*

STAR SCOOP!

One of the characters Selena loves to watch is Rachel on the TV show ***Friends***. When Selena met actor Jennifer Aniston, she said, "Rachel was my life!" As a kid, Selena tuned into ***Friends*** with her mom every week.

Jennifer Aniston

A FAMILIAR VOICE

For one of Selena's most famous roles, she never appeared on-screen! She voiced the role of Mavis, Dracula's daughter, in all four ***Hotel Transylvania*** films. Selena said she and Mavis have some things in common. "I think that Mavis cares a lot about her family, and she cares a lot about making sure that everyone's happy," Selena said. "I relate to her in that way. . . . I'm proud to have grown up with Mavis." Selena also voiced the roles of Helga in ***Horton Hears a Who!*** and a giraffe named Betsy in the movie ***Dolittle***.

STAR SCOOP!

Selena got the role of Betsy in ***Dolittle*** because the director's daughter was a big fan of hers! Selena loved the original movie, ***Dr. Dolittle***, as a kid, so she was happy to play the part.

AWARD-WINNING ACTING

Selena has won many awards for acting—and was nominated for even more! As of 2025, she had collected . . .

EMMY AWARDS: 1 NOMINATION

SCREEN ACTORS GUILD AWARDS: 1 WIN, 5 NOMINATIONS

TEEN CHOICE AWARDS: 3 WINS, 6 NOMINATIONS

PEOPLE'S CHOICE AWARDS: 4 WINS, 6 NOMINATIONS

GOLDEN GLOBE AWARDS: 4 NOMINATIONS

STAR SCOOP!

Selena set a Guinness World Record for most Nickelodeon Kids' Choice Awards won by an individual. She has won 13 Kids' Choice Awards for her work as an actor and musician. That's a lot of orange blimp trophies—and slime!

CHAPTER **3**

SINGING AND SONGWRITING

Selena didn't set out to be a singer. Acting was her first love, and singing was just a hobby! But her early acting roles involved a lot of singing, which she enjoyed. By age 16, Selena signed on with Hollywood Records, following in the footsteps of Disney stars **MILEY CYRUS** and **DEMI LOVATO**. Selena formed a pop-punk band called **Selena Gomez & The Scene**, and the band released three albums in only three years. That "hobby" turned into a career and turned the popular actor into a true pop star!

Selena and Blanco

STAR SCOOP!

In 2025, Selena released the album ***I Said I Love You First*** with Benny Blanco. Blanco is a record producer, and Selena and Blanco made their dating relationship public in 2023. Some of the album's songs are inspired by the couple's relationship.

SELENA'S SOLO SUCCESS

2013

July: *Stars Dance*, her first solo album, debuted at number one on the U.S. Billboard 200 chart.

August: Selena's "Come & Get It" video won the MTV Video Music Award for Best Pop Video.

August: Selena launched her *Stars Dance* world tour.

2015

Revival, her second solo album, debuted at number one.

2016

Selena launched her *Revival* world tour.

Selena won an American Music Award for Favorite Pop/Rock Female Artist.

2018

November: Selena became Spotify's most-streamed artist, with more than 46 million monthly listeners.

2019

October: Her song "Taki Taki" with DJ Snake won Song of the Year at the 2019 Latin American Music Awards.

November: Her single "Lose You to Love Me" hit number one on the Hot 100 list.

2020

Rare, Selena's third album, debuted at number one.

2021

She released *Revelación*, her first album sung in Spanish.

Revelación was nominated for a Grammy Award for Best Latin Pop Album.

2023

"Lose You to Love Me" reached 1 billion streams on Spotify.

2025

Selena released the album *I Said I Love You First* with Benny Blanco.

STAR SCOOP!

Selena's ***Stars Dance*** and ***Revival*** tours were both cut short because she was struggling with a disease called lupus. After getting a kidney transplant, her disease is "in remission," or under control.

quiz!

NAME THAT SONG

Guess which song goes with these popular lyrics!

1. "You promised the world and I fell for it.
I put you first and you adored it."

A. Love Me to Lose You
B. Love You to Love Me
C. Lose You to Love Me

2. "You got me like whoa, whoa, whoa . . ."

A. Calm Down
B. Get Down
C. Come Down

3. "I'm pickin' out this dress
Tryin' on these shoes . . ."

A. Singing Soon
B. Single Soon
C. Shopping Soon

4. "Your call has been forwarded to an automatic voice message system . . . "

A. Call Me
B. Call Me Back
C. Call Me When You Break Up

5. "We used to be close, but people can go from . . . "

A. People You Know
B. BFFs to Bros
C. Friends to Foes

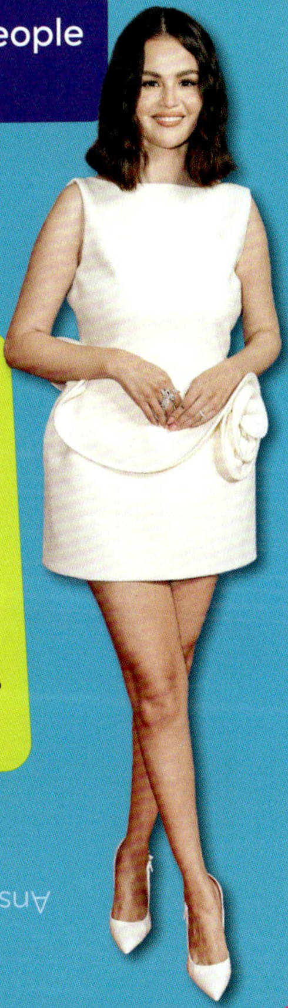

STAR SCOOP!

Selena cowrote "Lose You to Love Me" in only 45 minutes! It's about her breakup with Justin Bieber, but Selena says, "It's about more than a lost love. It's me learning to choose myself."

Answers: 1. C, 2. A, 3. B, 4. C, 5. A

TEAMING UP

Selena has made music with many talented musicians, such as . . .

DJ SNAKE AND CARDI B. FOR THE SONG "TAKI TAKI"

TAYLOR SWIFT DURING TAYLOR'S 1989 WORLD TOUR IN LOS ANGELES

COLDPLAY FOR THE SONG "LET SOMEBODY GO"

BLACKPINK FOR THE SONG "ICE CREAM"

GRACIE ABRAMS FOR THE SONG "CALL ME WHEN YOU BREAK UP"

CAMILO FOR THE SONG "999"

MARSHMELLO FOR THE SONG "WOLVES"

REMA FOR THE SONG "CALM DOWN"

KYGO FOR THE SONG "IT AIN'T ME"

BENNY BLANCO FOR THE ALBUM *I SAID I LOVE YOU FIRST*

Selena and Taylor

STAR SCOOP!

Selena and Taylor Swift are good friends. "Taylena" met when they were both dating members of the Jonas Brothers band. (Selena was dating Nick and Taylor was dating Joe.) When Selena turned 30, Taylor was her birthday date!

CHAPTER 4

A TALENTED PRODUCER

Selena does more than act on-screen. She's also a producer who manages the business side of TV shows and movies. Selena formed July Moon Productions when she was only 16 and went on to produce series such as ***13 Reasons Why***, ***Living Undocumented***, and ***Selena + Chef***. Selena started the cooking show in her own kitchen during the COVID pandemic. She invited a different chef for each episode, and they cooked and raised money for charity.

In 2024, she followed up with the spinoff ***Selena + Restaurant***. She films with celebrity chefs in their Los Angeles restaurants.

Selena on the set of *Selena + Chef*

STAR SCOOP!

Selena says of her own cooking skills, "They're not that great. I'm not gonna lie!" But she's learning!

"PRODUCE" YOUR OWN COOKING SHOW

Create a cooking show in your own kitchen, just like Selena. Here's how:

1. Come up with a name for your show, such as . . .

- **[Your first name] Mixes It Up**
- **The [your last name]'s Cook Nook**
- **[Your first name]'s Chop Shop**
- **The Snack Attack**
- **Sweets & Treats**

2. Invite a "guest chef" to join you. Maybe it's . . .

- **a friend**
- **a sister or brother**
- **an aunt**
- **a parent**
- **a grandparent**

- Choose a recipe to make together. Grilled cheese sandwiches? Chocolate chip cookies? Dog treats? Look for recipes online, or choose a favorite family recipe.

3. **Shoot a video. Record the most important steps, such as . . .**
    - **measuring ingredients**
    - **mixing them up**
    - **setting the timer on the stove or oven**

    (Ask an adult for help around hot appliances.)

4. While you cook, you can talk about causes that matter to you, just as Selena does. Do you love animals? Worry about the environment? Want to help families without homes? Talking about those issues raises awareness about them.

THE WIZARD RETURNS

What else has Selena produced? A spinoff of ***Wizards of Waverly Place***! Fans couldn't wait for the sequel, called ***Wizards Beyond Waverly Place***. The trailer had 69 million views in only ten days, making it Disney's most-watched trailer for a comedy series ever! Selena starred in her old role as Alex Russo in the first episode, which aired in late 2024. David Henrie came back as her brother Justin too. ***Wizards Beyond Waverly Place*** was the most-watched Disney Channel series premiere on Disney+.

STAR SCOOP!

Selena's sister Gracie inspired the sequel. Selena said she wanted to create "a whole new series for a new generation that families and people could watch, that my sister who is 11 could watch."

Selena and actor David Henrie attend the world premiere of *Wizards Beyond Waverly Place* in Los Angeles, California, in 2024.

CHAPTER **5**

BUSINESS SAVVY

Selena is smart when it comes to business. She partnered with some big fashion brands and invested money in companies she believes in. But her biggest project yet? That was starting Rare Beauty, her own cosmetics company. The company sells vegan makeup in recyclable packaging and never tests products on animals. The makeup comes in many shades to help people feel good about their own special traits.

People who buy **RARE BEAUTY** products can feel good about their purchases too. Why? Because one percent of all sales goes toward helping people struggling with mental health—a cause Selena is passionate about.

STAR SCOOP!

Selena Gomez is a billionaire, but most of her money didn't come from singing, acting, or producing. Eighty percent of it came from her Rare Beauty line!

THE FACE OF FASHION

Selena doesn't just love wearing the latest fashion trends. She helps promote some big brands too! They include:

Louis Vuitton gowns, jackets, bags, and even slippers!

Adidas Neo sneakers, shirts, skirts, bags, scarves, and beanies

Coach clothing and a "Selena Gomez" line of handbags

Puma "athleisure" collections—one inspired by rugby, one by ballet, and one called Strong Girl

La'Mariette swimwear in bright patterns and colors (to match Selena's personality!)

Kmart "Dream Out Loud" clothes and accessories made from earth-friendly materials

Selena wearing a Louis Vuitton dress at a fashion gala

STAR SCOOP!

Selena included positive messages when designing her bags for Coach. Quotes like "To be you is to be strong" and "Love yourself first" are printed on the bags, alongside Selena's handwritten signature!

THE SCOOP

What's Selena's most "delicious" business project so far? She is an owner and investor in the ice cream brand Serendipity! Selena was a fan of the **Serendipity 3** restaurant in New York City, so when they launched an ice cream line, she wanted in. But the ice cream is more than a sweet treat. With Selena as part owner, a percentage of all sales goes toward educating people about mental health. Selena is making a difference, one scoop at a time.

STAR SCOOP!

Selena helped create an ice cream flavor called Cookies & Cream Remix. The pink vanilla ice cream is swirled with fudge and chunks of chocolate sandwich cookies. Why is it pink? In honor of the song "Ice Cream" that Selena recorded with the band Blackpink!

Blackpink

serendipity
Cookies & Cream Remix
Pink Vanilla Ice Cream with Thick Fudge Swirl and Broken Cream-Filled Cookie Pieces

CHAPTER 6

THE CHANGE MAKER

Selena has been open with fans about having bipolar disorder, which affects her moods and emotions. She works hard to help others with mental health issues too. In 2020, Selena started the **RARE IMPACT FUND** to raise money and teach people about mental health. She and her mom also started **WONDERMIND**, a website focused on mental health.

Selena is grateful for the tough times she's gone through. "In a weird way," she said, "I turned the bad things into a good thing."

STAR SCOOP!

Since Selena started the Rare Impact Fund, she has raised millions of dollars to help 30 organizations across five continents. She turned her struggles into a *very* good thing!

LENDING A HAND THROUGH UNICEF

PERFORMED IN CHARITY CONCERTS TO RAISE MONEY

DONATED MONEY FOR VACCINATIONS DURING THE PANDEMIC

DESIGNED AND SOLD UNICEF T-SHIRTS AS PART OF HER DREAM OUT LOUD CLOTHING LINE

URGED FANS ON SOCIAL MEDIA TO DONATE TO UNICEF

TOOK PART IN CELEBRITY AUCTIONS BY SELLING HER OWN CLOTHING, INCLUDING A DRESS FROM A MUSIC VIDEO!

TRAVELED TO GHANA, CHILE, AND NEPAL TO SHINE A SPOTLIGHT ON CHILDREN IN NEED

APPEARED IN VIDEOS SHOWING HOW UNICEF HAS HELPED CHILDREN IN AFRICA

FOUGHT FOR CHILDREN AROUND THE WORLD TO BE ABLE TO GET VACCINES

WAS THE OFFICIAL SPOKESPERSON FOR UNICEF'S TRICK-OR-TREAT FUNDRAISER FOR KIDS—TWICE!

SCHOOLS FOR GIRLS

Selena wants to make sure that girls around the world get a good education. She lent her voice—literally—to narrate the documentary ***Girl Rising***, which focused on girls overcoming challenges to follow their dreams. Selena also worked with Step Up, an organization that gives girls the confidence to go after college educations. And Selena partnered with **WE CHARITY** to raise money to build schools for girls in Kenya. Selena isn't only a role model for young girls—she raises money and her voice to empower them. Go, Selena!

STAR SCOOP!

Selena traveled to Kenya to visit the schools she'd helped raise the funds to build. When she came back home, she said, "A part of my heart is still in Kenya."

Selena poses with students at a WE Charity event in California in 2018.

DESIGN A T-SHIRT (LIKE SELENA!)

Selena designed T-shirts to raise money for UNICEF. What cause do you care about? Design a T-shirt to support it! Here's how:

- Get a white T-shirt and fabric markers.
- Think of a cause that matters to you. Are you passionate about protecting animals? Taking care of the environment? Raising money to help find a cure for a disease or illness?
- Come up with a message for the front of your T-shirt. Maybe it's "Paws for a Cause" or "Make Today Earth Day."
- Add some graphics, patterns, or pictures that have to do with your cause. Can you add paw prints on the sleeves? Ocean waves along the hemline? A big heart in the center?

ABOUT THE AUTHOR

Erin Falligant has written more than 50 books for children. Her Joss series for American Girl, written about a young surfer with hearing loss, earned a 2020 Moonbeam Gold Medal Award. Erin draws from her master's degree in child clinical psychology to write advice books on changing bodies, standing up to bullies, making friends, and mastering mindfulness. To learn more about Erin and her books, visit www.erinfalligant.com.

READ MORE ABOUT YOUR FAVORITE STARS!

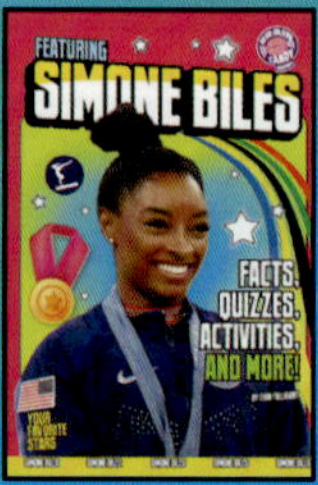